7 Simple Steps to a Healthier, Happier **YOU**

Katie Lowndes

Balboa Press books may be ordered through booksellers or by contacting:

Balboa Press
A Division of Hay House
1663 Liberty Drive
Bloomington, IN 47403
www.balboapress.com.au
1 (877) 407-4847

Interior Image Credit:
Artwork by: Claire Orrell
Illustration by: Bima Perera

ISBN: 978-1-5043-1975-1 (sc)
ISBN: 978-1-5043-1976-8 (e)

Print information available on the last page.

Balboa Press rev. date: 11/27/2019

BALBOA.PRESS
A DIVISION OF HAY HOUSE

CONTENTS

INTRODUCTION

Over the last 8 years, I have been sub-consciously researching and trying different things in order to reach the point of writing this book.

These simple steps help me to become more energetic, healthier, and happier when I feel unbalanced.
Life is harder now even though we have so much more at our fingertips. However, with each new development, we are faced with new challenges. We can be anything, do anything, because we have so much choice.

Food is delivered to our door in record time, we can book a taxi with the touch of a button, and said taxi can arrive in 2 minutes, money travels throughout the globe at the snap of your fingers, and we don't even need to leave the house to shop. It's amazing and daunting.

Do you ever feel overwhelmed by the options and pressures? What diet is better for you? Organic, vegan, vegetarian, keto, fasting, or paleo? What about exercise? F45, CrossFit, kettlebells, Pilates, yoga?
The aforementioned advancements are fantastic in their own right, so it seems ridiculous that they could stress us out, but they do. Life can become manic and overwhelming at times!

My Aussie fella—now husband—Luke and I moved to Australia in 2011. From the grey skies of the UK to the blue skies of Melbourne, the change was exciting.

My positive attitude ensured I never dwelled on the stresses that come with a big move. This glass-half-full mentality allowed me to tackle the shift from everything I knew. Luke's family and friends embraced me, and I never had to feel lonely.

Of course, over time I met new people through work and friends. Working from home can be a challenge as you are not able to connect with others face-to-face and you must be disciplined. So, it's no surprise that I receded into myself. I call this the Monkey Mind: Overanalyzing everything and questioning whether this is the right job for me or should I start a new business, and am I happy?

My positivity did not allow me to acknowledge that I found making new friends, finding new work, and learning everything all over again challenging. The new shops, new phrases, new roads, new transport, new holiday days, and events were overwhelming. I always had to be at my best when meeting new people as first impressions count.

As I aged, I became picky and making new friends was tiresome. Your long-term friends and family understand you, while new friends and acquaintances do not know your history and the path that took you to where you are today.

What I didn't know then but do now is that it's ok not to be ok.

I enjoyed food more than I should have and consumed wine at celebrations, to relax, and as a crutch. As I aged, I became aware of my health and diet, but losing the pounds became a challenge. After over 17 years of being in the beauty industry, and a natural interest in health, wellness, and diet, I became acutely aware of how what we eat and drink, and how we exercise can affect our mind and body.

In January 2014, I rescued my little dog Max and he brought a lot of love into our lives. Walking him every morning became one of the best habits I adopted, and my morning feels incomplete without a walk. The little steps and habits help to support our mind and body.

I had—and have—an amazing life, as do you, but sometimes the daily grind becomes too much.

You may already be aware of the topics discussed in this book, but sometimes we need a little nudge to remind ourselves.

I hope that my little stories and poems make you smile and this book comes to your aid when you are having a tough time. We all need time to rest and recuperate.

So, that's enough about me and the why, let's look at how you can live a happier, healthier life.

Xx

Step One – Clean

The environment you live and work in impacts how you feel. If you are surrounded by mess, dusty old books, unfiled papers, and cluttered wardrobes, then guess what? Your mind is also cluttered. If you are holding on to certain items for nostalgic reasons or because you 'might need it', this is the danger zone.

This journey begins here. Clean up, de-clutter, and get organised!

General

Eliminate the clutter on shelves—it just makes for extra cleaning and gathers dust. We tend to accumulate *stuff* that adds nothing to our lives.

My grandma displayed her collection of Wedgewood China on shelves but never used a piece. What a waste of time, effort, and money that was. If you don't use it, you don't need it.

Bedroom

Are you holding on to unnecessary amounts of bed sheets and duvet covers? You know the ones: old ones that have bobbles, ones that don't match the current designs in the house, and sheets that fit old mattress sizes. I had one with a large, ink stain from a rogue Sharpie!

Keep 2-3 changes of sheets and duvets for your bed and a set or two for your spare bed. The rest of them? Be gone!

TIP: Get pillow protectors to place under the pillowcase, especially if you have white sheets, as they ensure your pillows last longer and don't yellow, which is so attractive…

'The Chair' (or the Bermuda Triangle)

Do you stack worn clothes or stuff that you need to put away on a chair? Is the mess a massive mound of dirty things you swear you will put away? Have you lost items recently? Do you ever sit on the chair? You probably can't because it's covered with crap. If the chair is clean and you *still* don't sit on it, simply get rid of it.

Wardrobe and Clothes Drawers

Does each item of clothing you own fit? Is it ever likely to fit? If the answer is no, I am sorry, but is time to say goodbye and RIP.

Have you moved from house-to-house with items of clothing you love and never wear? Well, it's time for them to go too.

I once owned this beautiful pair of trousers, which moved everywhere with me, and saying goodbye was hard but it's harder to try them on year after year only to realise they *still* don't fit.

Do you have anything worn, torn, faded, bobbly, or coats with broken zips?

Do you have shoes you love but never wear because they are uncomfortable? Have you ever worn them? You know what I'm going to suggest by now…

Knickers and socks with holes, loose threads, and fading, and thongs/g-strings you've never worn? They all take up unnecessary space.

Hang what you can and roll up the rest in your drawers so you can see each item. Less clothing means less mess when you're trying to find something to wear.

Grabbing the first thing you see—and wearing it over and over—is tempting, so minimalise your clothing for the sake of variety.

Bathroom

Throw out any unused or old products. Skincare products have a 3-year shelf life and 6 months opened.

Lipsticks accumulated over ten years are bound to be full of bacteria (and probably don't smell too great) and eyeshadows have collected oils from using your fingertips to apply on the eyelid. Cringe. Always try and use an applicator or clean brush for application so that the eyeshadow does not become hard and shiny.

Makeup brushes can harbour bacteria if they are not cleaned regularly, and this bacteria is spread over your skin each day you use the brush.

You don't need 50 body washes, moisturisers, hand creams, and hair products so, think about the ones you use regularly and try not to let flashy adverts tempt you. If you don't know what gives you the required results, now is the time to find out!

As a side note, what do your skincare products contain? You want to be careful with what you are putting on your face and body, so think clean, recyclable, and sustainable.

Once you have gone through your products, organise them into bags. I have a bag for hair accessories and pins, one for personal care items, one for makeup, and one for first aid. Everything has a place, so I never have to rummage around.

Avoid SLS, SLES, Parabens, DEA, and Mineral Oil as a start.

Kitchen

This place is a danger zone! Unused tools, old cutlery, utensils overflowing draws, clutter on benches, biscuit tins, bread bins, tea boxes, cookie jars, out-of-date herb tins at the back of your pantry… *Arggggh.*

I use boxes for flours, sugars, and nuts to organise my pantry. After having a weevil outbreak, I am conscious of open containers in the cupboard as they could become a feeding frenzy if one little weevil gets in. Trust me, it isn't pretty.

TIP: Silicone lids that stretch over the mouth of jars or seal the end of cut lemons, peppers, and other vegetables are a great reusable alternative. They keep the vegetable sealed without the use of cling film or foil and reduce the number of plates floating around the fridge. And they last a lifetime.

Also, try beeswax wraps to keep your bread, cheese, and anything else you can think of, they keep items fresher for longer and are a more sustainable way of storing items.

Have you accumulated a ridiculous amount of mugs? I think people buy them as presents because I ended up with a whole box that I just donated to the Salvation Army. I mean, how many mugs does one girl need? I've kept a few special mugs and the matching set. So, I have about ten in total. I think I *had* about 40!

The same principle applies to glasses. I now keep our wine and spirit glasses in a special cupboard. Our everyday tumblers are kept in the pantry with the mugs and we have a set of cheap glasses for events in a box in the garage. We try to avoid plastic cups—for environmental reasons. The drink tastes bad out of plastic anyway.

The same rules that apply in the kitchen apply to everywhere else, really. Banish unused, old, rusty, cracked, and broken items.

Living Room

CDs! DVDs! Who still has them? Some people like to keep them because they still watch them.

We were the same, so I put them into CD wallets. It takes up no space, they are all in one place, and they don't collect dust. They just sit in the tv unit, not cluttering up shelves and taking up space.

Ornaments. Are they necessary? Or are they clutter? Keep counter tops and side tables clear. I am not saying to rid yourself of character, I'm just saying you don't need ten ornaments on every table.

Office

You might not have an office, but most homes tend to have a study space. The best things I have in my office is a little filing cupboard for papers, and a box in the draw for pens.

Try not to accumulate old writing books and magazines, papers or miscellaneous items that you actually never use of refer back to. Ask yourself two questions: Is it necessary? and do you use it?

It's important to keep personal papers and documents filed as you never know when you may need them—for example, new passports, mortgages, and tax purposes. I am aware of the importance of this after changing my name after marriage and the Visa applications over the years. It's stressful if you can't find them when asked, and even more so when you have to get new ones issued.

My husband's office is terrible, I'll be honest. It drives me mad. He carries this set of papers to action around the house with him. They end up on the kitchen table, the kitchen bench, living room side table, and his office couch is another favourite location. You can feel my frustration! Action and file the papers or bin them. Carrying these papers around is like carrying a weighted to-do list on his shoulders.

Garage

Alright, I'm feeling smug right now. The Salvation Army just picked up a load of old, unused furniture, rugs, cutlery, and crockery. It was a relief and created so much space! We are also giving these items to those who need them.

I now have cleaner shelves, a box for tools, space for filed, annual tax papers, and as I I sell some items online I have a clean and clear display unit so that I can see my stock. Everything has a home. I also know where everything is so I don't feel stressed.

In reality, it didn't take long. We imagine this massive task, but once you get going it can be done in no time. You have to be quick, and a little ruthless, and afterwards you feel lighter and in control.

Hygge

Now, it's all well and good being clean and tidy, but you don't want to be living in a hospital! You need to add some elements of warmth and that's when a little bit of *hygge* comes in.

I thought it was pronounced High-Ga, but it could be hue-gah or Hhyooguh. According to *The Little Book of Hygge,* the Danish way of living involves low lights for the evening, twinkling candles, cozy throws on the couch, and the feeling of happiness in general. Basically, *hygge* refers to anything that makes you feel snuggly and homely. If you are picking candles, make sure you avoid paraffin bases. Beeswax-based candles are the healthiest, but they do come with a higher price tag. I use these for the glow and use a diffuser for aroma.

Feng Shui

From what I know, *feng shui* is the positioning of everything in your home to make the most out of the earth's energy (chi). Clutter disrupts this flow, creating negative energy.

Interestingly, the most important aspects are de-cluttering, adding plants, clearing obstacles, and ensuring the windows and doors are clean. *Feng shui* has a lot to do with placement, colour, materials, and textures, and if it's something that interests you, consider talking to a consultant or reading a good book.

A happy, healthy, clean, and fresh home makes for a happier you. Your home should be a haven, somewhere you feel safe and relaxed.

Step 2 – Monkey Mind

Monkey Mind

Who's that monkey on my mind?
Telling me I can't do stuff all the time

You tell me I'm not good enough
And that I should lose weight

Actually, I'm pretty tough
And I look kinda great

Stop holding me back
I won't take your crap

I like being happy
Not stressed and snappy
I choose what I listen too and that's not you
Don't make me brood
I'll choose my own mood

Now I just smile, it lights up my face
I think happy thoughts and I'm in a good
place.

Even as I write this, that little monkey has been jumping all over the place! All morning. The result is procrastination rather than writing this book.

We talk so much about our diet and exercise, but maybe not enough about the mind. Luckily, meditation and mindfulness aren't only words for hippies. The other thing I noticed when it comes to mental health is that there is a stigma around seeing a counsellor or psychologist, yet no one questions seeing a personal trainer.

Baggage collects in our brain over the years, stories that we turnover again and again. These change and become entirely *new* stories and something small can often become something *big* and harmful.

Talking can be difficult to friends or relatives. You may feel like you can't open up to friends about certain aspects of your life that are upsetting you because you don't want to seem like a winge. Alternatively you may feel the need to confide about a friend, relative or partner but feel like you can't as that would be a betrayal to them and you don't wish for them to be seen in a different light.

Why not get everything out of your head? You will feel lighter and that small thing won't develop into something big. Tackle the dramas, the conversations, emails, or interactions that are on your mind. Face the worries and talk them through, let them free and they won't weigh you down.

Of course, you don't necessarily need to talk to someone, there are other methods you could try before that.

I recommend journaling. You could do this when you wake up or before you go to bed. I say either because sometimes I do both or one or the other.

The idea behind journalling is to dump your head on a page. Once it's dumped, it's no longer monkeying around, evolving, growing, and replaying. Just get it out of your head, take an action towards sorting out whatever it might be.

Yesterday morning, I received an email that riled me. There was no direct attack on me and it wasn't really a big deal, but for some reason it ruined my morning. But then I sat, re-read the email, and addressed it in a non-defensive way. I soon realised that there was no reason for me to be upset in the first place! It really was ridiculous. Sometimes we are just wired to jump to a certain conclusion. If I hadn't addressed this straight away it would have grown and developed throughout the day and I may have even gone to bed with it rolling around my mind festering. Either address the situation, and if you can't, write one or three pages. Just write and empty. If you do this you may find a solution quickly, look at something from a different perspective, and if before bed then you won't spend the night tossing and turning.

The second tool I use is planning. Do you ever feel overwhelmed because of a long list of tasks? Work, children, pets, home, admin, travel… the list goes on and on.

I like to write out what is happening each day and then note a list of tasks that can be added across the week. Sometimes, I write the list next to the weekly plan and then you know when you have a spare minute you can tick it off. Nine times out of ten, I end up doing the list straight away and then it's done! Obsolete! The euphoria of ticking off that list is amazing.

Have you heard of the book *Eat The Frog*? In a nutshell, it is about doing the hardest, most annoying task first and then the rest of the tasks seem easy. I used to leave the hardest tasks until last because I didn't *really* want to complete them. I now do the same thing. The progress is phenomenal!But prioritising can be tough. Prioritise yourself *first*. Sometimes I find that I do things for others first as I don't want to let them down, but then I am essentially prioritising everyone over me and then I don't have energy left for *my* things. Hence, taking 8 years to write this book.

There is one other thing I'd like you to do. I'd like you to write a list of all the things in your life that stress you out. Now, let's be clear, there is always going to be something that you may not want to do and have to do, but if possible why not eliminate or outsource. For example, we now get our shopping delivered, which means we spend less time and money buying food. It frees up time for us to focus on other things, like spending time with friends. Take a look at what you can change or outsource in your life to free up time for what's important to you. That could be spending time with your children or having some time for some self-care.

I mentioned the fact that we are wired to react or think in certain ways. These are learned behaviours, formed from years of reactions and thoughts. It can be hard to change and reset these behaviours but it can be done.

Gratitude

A simple step to achieving gratitude and feeling positive, is to write three things that you are grateful for in the morning. Putting your mind in this grateful mode will put a smile on your face and *wire* you to be happy. You can be grateful for the sun, a person, a memory, anything really and this can set you up for a positive day.

Depression and Anxiety

I am no expert in this field, but if you are feeling down, can't sleep, or, alternatively, want to sleep all the time, have been feeling low for an extended period of time, anything longer than the normal ups and downs, please seek advice! It is better to be safe than sorry. Please see your doctor or call the following numbers. The brain is a complicated thing and sometimes a chemical imbalance or hormone problems can affect our mental state. The point is, you don't have to live like this, so please seek advice.

The demands of everyday life can be overwhelming: technology, work, children, trying to be fit, healthy, work hard, cook, food shop, clean, socialise, have fun, rest... Thoughts run through your head and you can get yourself in a spin. You may find yourself waking up with anxiety, or maybe you can't even get to sleep due to these demands.

Stress, and the causes, are different for everyone, but the one thing that you can feel comforted about is that we have all felt the same at some point. I think we feel that admitting that we are stressed or anxious makes us weak or that talking about it will effect others in a negative way. It is important to realise that it's ok to feel this way and talking about it is really important and cathartic.

How are you dealing with stress? Think about it and be honest.

https://www.beyondblue.org.au
1300224636

https://www.mentalhealth.org.uk
http://depressionuk.org

https://www.mind.org.uk
0300 123 3393

Gratitude

A little daily gratitude
And having the right attitude

Can stop you feeling crappy
Instead you'll feel real happy

Sending positive vibes
Brings energy in tribes

Sending out love
Clears clouds from above

So, take some time everyday
To be thankful in any way

Step 3 – Diet

We eat three times a day, so our life is full of food. Eating it, buying it, cooking it, planning it...
It can be quite a headache if you don't enjoy cooking or are not particularly a "foodie". I hope these quick tips on diet and planning make your life a little easier, healthier, and enjoyable.

Food is our fuel and affects our energy levels, mood, general health, and, in fact, could make us very sick, so it's important we choose wisely.

You wouldn't put diesel in a petrol car, so why do we fill ourselves with fuel that is bad for us?

To me there are a few quick and easy wins: avoid added colours, flavours and preservatives.

Read the labels on the food you buy can be scary. Some companies even put on the front of the packaging, *No Colours or Flavours*, and then you turn it over and it is full of preservatives. Some food marketed as healthy or low fat is packed full of additives and e numbers.The less something is tampered with the better it is, in my opinion! I'm not saying I'm perfect. In desperate times, you sometimes have to eat what is there and you just do your best to have the cleanest option.

Organic is best, but it's expensive—sometimes nearly double! However, farmers markets, and there are now home delivery services that have great value veg and fruit boxes.

The Environmental Working group in the US developed a list called the Dirty Dozen. A list of fruit and vegetables that contain the most Pesticides, so if anything try and buy these in Organic form.

1. Strawberries
2. Spinach
3. Kale
4. Nectarines
5. Apples
6. Grapes
7. Peaches
8. Cherries
9. Pears
10. Tomatoes
11. Celery
12. Potatoes

If you do eat meat and fish, I am very conscious of what is healthier for you but also what is better for the environment. For meat, opt for grass fed and free range/organic. In addition, you can choose sustainably sourced fish.

Everyone has different dietary needs and beliefs are different, such as vegan, vegetarian, paleo, and pescatarian. I eat red meat once a week and stick to chicken or fish and vegetarian nights for the rest of the week. The choice is really entirely up to you. We have certainly increased our vegetarian meals and decreased red meat intake.

Everyone's body is different and will react and behave differently to different diets. The key is to listen to your own body and notice how it changes when you are eating different diets. When does your energy drop? How does your mood change? What about your bowel movements? Weight gain or loss? Skin, hair and nails? All of these signs tell us what is doing us good or bad. Government guidelines are good to follow, but if you are unsure or have particular health issues then please see your doctor or dietician for advice.

Meal Planning

One of the biggest keys to success is planning. I hate the question, 'what's for dinner?'. It makes me stress! If you don't plan, you end up over shopping or purchasing last minute takeaway. You might end up with lots of leftover food too. Plan ahead, use items over multiple meals—e.g. use a bunch of coriander in two meals, so it doesn't end up floppy and unuseable.

Planning takes away stress, lowers costs, and increases health. WIN.

My family started coming up with a weekly plan, but now we use a 3-week rotating plan, so that we aren't overeating the same meals. It keeps meals interesting. You can, of course, change your 3-week plan in the seasons to make the most of seasonal produce and tailor the meals to cooler or warmer climates.

I plan 5 meals a week as we tend to go out, have a takeaway or eat leftovers one night, but you can do whatever suits your lifestyle. We write up the meal plans and, at the side of each week, write the ingredients for shopping. This way your meals and shops are planned.

Shopping

Whether you do or don't have kids, shopping can be stressful. I now find that I need to go to several different shops to get the produce I need. Whether you are busy with work or children, there are easier ways.

Most supermarkets now deliver. We get organic veg and dairy products delivered from Ceres. They reuse the boxes and bottles that their products are delivered in and we know we are getting the best local and seasonal produce.

Whatever I can't get at Ceres, I get at the supermarket where we also purchase any household goods needed. They also deliver. Both orders get delivered on the same day and I find buying online means I spend less time and money on shopping and don't end up buying extra, unnecessary things.

Herbs

I grow fresh herbs on our roof terrace and balcony. Obviously, some last longer through the winter than others, like thyme, rosemary, mint, and oregano, and some are a bit more sensitive, like basil and coriander. If I have to buy herbs, I tend to use as much as I can across the meals for the week and then I like to use the leftover herbs to make chimichurri or basil and garlic oil. These last a few weeks and can be used as dressing for salads, meat, fish, pastas, soups, and anything else your imagination can come up with. This way they are never wasted and you always have a tasty go-to sauce in the fridge.

Storage

Storing your products correctly is important. Wrapping things in cling film, foil or tins with caps doesn't help the environment or the produce. I now wrap everything in beeswax wraps, which makes it last longer. I store onion and avocado in specific boxes, and use huggys to seal the end of fruit and vegetables, like lemon or peppers.

Freezer

The simple act of freezing can help save money and also provide quick wins in the kitchen. Freezing bread rather than binning it once it becomes dry is my first tip. Fresh bread is so tasty, but we all know that after a few days it's not so great. Before it goes from dry to mouldy freeze it. By freezing the bread, you always have some toast to hand . In addition to this I always have peas, spinach, berries, breaded chicken (free range and free of colours flavours and preservatives), left over gravy or stock handy for last minute dinners. I must admit there are some potato gems and a frozen pizza for desperate times when I may be sick or suffering from a hangover!

Food can affect your mood
Get too hungry, you may brood
Try no additives, preservatives or flavours
As these can affect your behaviour

Food should give you energy and make
you feel happy
Not unhealthy, sluggish, and like a fatty

Eat the colors of the rainbow in your veg
Five portions a day is your pledge
And maybe a little treat
Something sweet
Once a week

Remember to stay hydrated
Two litres a day is the way
Maybe a herbal tea or two
Room temp for your digestion
That is my suggestion

You are what you eat
From your head to your feet

Choose well and you'll feel swell

Alcohol

I grew up in an era where Friday night meant the school would descend to the local park and bus stops and walk the streets causing mayhem while drinking White Lightning, Lambrini, or Ravers. Your tipple depended on what cash you had and how hardcore you were.

Everyone's relationship with alcohol is different and in some ways this relationship started very early on in your life and is almost habitual. I remember when new neighbours moved in next door and they invited the local neighbourhood over to say Hi. The family got ready, bringing wine as a gift. Dad got excited about a party, and looked forward to making new friends and having some fun. We knocked on the door, handing over our gift, which they politely declined as they were practising teetotalism. I'll never forget my dad's face! Let's just say we did not hang around long at said party. He grew up in an era where if you didn't drink then you weren't fun.

I drink to celebrate wins, and to have fun with friends over dinner or out at the pub. I also like to have a drink to wind down and relax. I'm sure this resonates with some of you. It's been a hard day and you immediately think, 'I could murder a glass of wine'. Which in itself is a ridiculous saying! How on earth do you murder a glass of wine? I suppose, shoving it down your throat would work.

I love sipping wine whilst cooking dinner, bedding down to watch a cheesy romcom on Netflix when my husband is away. It's almost a ritual. He's away, so wine, romcom and chicken wings is how I spend my night. The problem with this is, what if you have a week where the workdays are stressful and then you have celebrations with friends on the weekend? Before you know it, you could be drinking every day! That is simply not good for the mind or the body.

We now live in Australia, but I am from the UK, which means we travel back every year for about a month and visit all of my friends, family, and work colleagues, and spend every day catching up, celebrating, and holidaying. After a month of that you really see and feel the effects. When I return from holiday, I have gained weight, there is more fluid in my body as it is trying to fight the toxicity of alcohol (aka cellulite) and my mind is just not firing to its full potential.

I'm really conscious about alcohol and, at one point, downloaded the Drinkaware app and tracked my alcohol habits. It's a great way to keep your intake in check. I also have months where I have NO BOOZE, which is actually easier than saying, 'ok, you can drink a bit on weekends'. This might just work for me, but it seems to work more when I go all in. Of course, you could just give up altogether! I have contemplated it and I know people who have done this successfully.

I like to stick to a max of three drinks in one sitting and not exceed the advice given by government guidelines: no more than 6 x 175ml glasses of wine a week, 6 pints of beer or the equivalent in spirits, which is 14 x 25ml measures.

There is, of course, the peer pressure aspect to think about: 'Come on, have a drink', 'don't be boring', 'Come on, we haven't seen you for ages, have a drink with me', 'I don't want to drink alone', etc. You can give in and the next day you will feel worse for giving in and, of course, the natural after-alcohol-effects of anxiety kicks in. Sometimes it is best not to say anything at all. Just get your own drinks. No one needs to know what you are drinking and, at the end of the day, if they can't support you then are they really a friend?

A few key facts courtesy of The Truth About Alcohol – NETFLIX.

1. There is evidence linking cancer and alcohol
2. Alcohol related liver diseases; alcohol causes inflammation in the liver
3. When drinking, your balance and hand-eye coordination is affected
4. You lose self-control
5. Alcohol numbs pain; we feel warmer when we are actually losing heat
6. Alcohol makes you hungry

7. The more water you have in your body the less drunk you will feel, which is why a smaller person tends to become inebriated quicker

8. Alcohol is absorbed in the small intestine not the large intestine, so if you eat it takes longer to reach there. Eating prior to drinking helps to cut food cravings

New Government Alcohol Guidelines for Men and Women

You shouldn't regurlary drink more then **14 units a week**

This means you should not drink more than this amount of...

Wine - Standard size of 175 ml

...**Or** this amount of **lager** or **ale** - Standard size of 568 ml

...**Or** this amount of **cider** - Standard size of 568 ml

...**Or** this amount of **spirit** - Standard size of 25 ml

According to UK government guidelines 2019. Please visit Drinkaware.co.uk for more information.

An Ode to Alcohol

A little bit of wine is fine,
One seven five ml is the standard,
Six of these a week being the peak.

Maybe not in one sitting,
This may be slightly off putting,
You may struggle to get out of bed,
and will have a sore head.

If you are trying to shred,
Ditch the booze,
You'll struggle to lose,
If you can't pass this test,
Then a cheeky VLS is best.

Step 4 – Exercise

Now I'm not a PT (personal trainer) and I'm also not a particular 'fan' of exercising.

What I do know is this:

I feel better when I have exercised;

It's hard to get started;

I'm a yoyo; sometimes I'm really in to it, other times I'm not;

I know that every time I start something else becomes a habit and I do better (so, keep trying);

When I'm on a roll and in the zone, it feels great;

I run weird (think Phoebe in *Friends*);

I have limited muscles, to put it politely;

At times I have attended classes and probably did more harm than good as I have been performing the exercises wrong (hence, weak muscles in places, and aches and pains in others).

Now, there are quite a few negatives there and I am sure some of you can relate. There are so many different choices, just like with dieting. It's hard to know where to start and what is going to be best for you.

I suppose the key is to do what you enjoy the most and just do *something*! With desk jobs on the rise, working from home and the ease or transport like UBER, movement can be limited. If you can, try to use public transport and walk up stairs instead of taking lifts.

It's amazing how going for a walk can get the juices flowing. By that, I mean your energy. Sometimes it's hard to move when you wake up, especially if it's cold and dark, but just like airing out a stuffy room, you need to air out yourself too.

I am lucky to have my little, furbaby Max. Every day I have to get up and walk him. When I first brought him home it was a bit of a struggle, but 5 years down the track I feel the need to walk for me too. Even when I am away without him, I still feel the need to get up, go out, and stretch my weary legs. It lifts the cobwebs, gets my chi flowing around the body, oxygen in the lungs, and my brain wakes up.

I've tried spinning, yoga, HIIT, Body Balance, kettlebells, Body Pump, running, Pilates, Zumba, PT, swimming, and, at times, I have enjoyed all of them.

The key is to find out what fits in with your life. What is easy to get to? What fits in your budget? What about time? Do you have time to go on your lunch hour or before or after work? What is enjoyable enough that you will stick to it? Also, listen to your body.

Right now, I enjoy Reformer Pilates. This class has helped to retrain my muscle groups and tone my body at the same time. The class times work for my schedule; the class is not even a 5 minute walk from my house and I enjoy the music. I do this a couple of times a week. In addition to this, I am trying to run a couple of times a week using my 5K Runner app and my running soundtrack. Even though I don't think I am a particularly good runner, I can get this done in 25 minutes, and it increases my heart rate, I get to run around the beautiful gardens nearby, and I can do it at a time that suits.

Whatever you choose, make sure it's not difficult to get to. You may have already commuted to work that day, so why commute just to stay fit? Make the most of the hours in a day; they should not be spent sittng in a car, train, tram or bus.

As I said earlier, it can be hard to stick to and sometimes we start and stop. The key is to keep trying and you will slowly form new habits (like my morning walk).

If you are experiencing pains in certain places, you may need some help from a doctor, a physiotherapist or a PT, as you, like me, may have been doing things incorrectly. For example, one half of my body was doing all of the hard work and I would inadvertently use my chest muscle instead of my bicep when lifting. Listen to your body and think about whether you need some extra help or guidance from a professional.

Exercise

F45, CrossFit, Pilates, yoga

How to decide

What's your vibe

Pop on your Fitbit

Make a new habit

Get in those steps

And maybe a few reps

Just get moving

It's been proven

That you'll feel great

And will get in shape

Do what's fun

Maybe that's a run

You have a choice

Listen to your voice

Dance, swim, play

What's in your way?

What better way to start your day

Step 5 - Beauty

What's in an age,
It's only a stage,
You may feel creaky and saggy,
Your comfy pants no longer baggy.

You take a look in the mirror at your face,
To see your mum in its place.

You are, of course, wiser,
Some would say a survivor,
Of lifes little ups and downs,
Have been at crossroads,
Maybe have kissed a few toads!

So, how can we age gracefully,
Live longer and happily?

10,000 steps a day they say,
With five portions of fruit and veg a day,

Cleanse, tone, moisturise and don't
forget SPF,
This will give you fresh skin and prevent
the sag,
No one wants to look like a leather bag.

Don't take yourself too seriously,
Live wild and carefree,
Travel and explore,
Find new places you adore.

Surround yourself with good friends,
Don't get too hung up on trends,
Ignore the monkey mind,
He is sometimes very unkind.

Smile, love, laugh, dance, sing, create,
Be in your happy state!

My love affair with beauty started in my mum's bathroom back in England. I grew up in Stocksfield, a beautiful village in Northumberland. The bathroom had peach tiles and gold taps; a little bit of 80s glamour! I loved going in to mum's en suite because the different lotions and potions were so enticing.

It was in the peach bathroom that mum taught me about the three-step system: cleanse, tone, and moisturise. Of course, I couldn't afford the products that she used, but I started to take care of my skin from this day on and had a passion for beauty. I am blessed with soft skin, but was not so blessed with often congested skin.

Since moving to Australia and receiving many a compliment about my 'lovely English skin', I now appreciate the lack of sun damage and understand how the strong Australian sun can affect the skin. (My husband has had three basal cell carcinomas removed.)

From the age of 18, I noticed cellulite creeping in. 18? WHY? Fast forward to age 21, after working on cruise ships, I suddenly noticed I had varicose veins. My poor legs were falling apart and that was then, I am now 37!

None of us are perfect and wouldn't life be dull if we were? So, here are my top tips for maintaining healthy skin and body.

Skin and Body care

1. Choose wisely! Avoid products with chemicals, parabens, SLES, SLS, DEAs, and mineral oils.
2. It's up to you and your beliefs whether you choose organic or not. I use and work with ELEMIS. They use both Organic, Botanical and Marine extracts and are conscious about nasty ingredients. In addition they use science and technology to get results which I love and appreciate as I am getting older.
3. Make sure the brands you use do not test on animals.

4. If you are going to pay good money for skincare, do not forget your body. So many times I see people with beautiful moisturisers for the face, but then they use some cheap, chemical wash for their body.

5. Make sure you remove all of your makeup at night, and, if you aren't wearing any, it is still the best time to cleanse as you may have been in pollution all day or have inadvertently touched your face.

6. Cleanse, tone, and moisturise morning and night and consider exfoliating a couple of times a week to remove any dead skin cells, followed by a treatment mask to give you a boost. This will assist with cell turnover and the penetration of your moisturisers, serums and oils.

7. See an expert! Ask for some advice from a beauty therapist or Aesthetician for what is best for your skin. You may think you are dry, but you may just be dehydrated. Also, you could be over-stripping your skin.

8. Don't forget your eyes, neck, and décolleté. These are the key areas where ageing shows the most.

9. I prefer skincare that works with my skins natural functions rather than damaging or stripping it. Hence using ELEMIS.

10. Use a body brush in the morning to increase circulation and remove dead skin cells before you shower. Always brush towards the heart and use quick and firm strokes on dry skin over the legs and arms, and in a circular motion over the belly.

Body Brush diagram

11. Apply moisturiser/oil. I like to use a detox oil as I have concerns with cellulite. I see a massive improvement in cellulite when I avoid alcohol , increase water intake and use my brush and oil together.

12. Makeup is an extension of your skincare so please be mindful of ingredients. I like to use a mineral makeup (Jane Iredale is my favourite). Also, make sure you regularly and gently clean your brushes with shampoo. I work the brush in a circular motion in the palm of my hand with the shampoo and then gently rinse clean.

13. Wear broad spectrum SPF every day at a minimum of 30. Broad spectrum covers the UVA (ultraviolet A-rays) (According to the Cancer Council UVA accounts of 95% of rays that hit Earth, responsible for ageing and strong links to cancer) and B-rays. A = ageing, B = burning. UVC does not reach Earth as the ozone absorbs it.

14. Of course, diet is key for good skin. You will often see problems in your skin because of a bad diet, alcohol or stress. So, eat well and drink plenty of water!

Cellulite
You really bite
Since you entered my life
My body is in strife

I'm not ready for this jelly
Please don't head to my belly
You started on my thighs
Please hear my cries
Now I see you on my arms
You're giving me sweaty palms

I know the solution
The cellulite revolution
Body Brush every morning
Toxins, this is your warning
Gonna break you down
You'll soon drown
Two litres of water a day is the way

Now, fat cells its your turn
Time for you to burn
Have to exercise every day
In whatever way

Something I like,
Walk swim or hike
This will make me feel good
Will improve my mood

Jelly or no jelly
Belly or no belly
I want to be happy
Not snappy

I choose health and happiness
Not feeling down and in distress
So, if I see a little jelly
Even on my belly
I'm not going to punish myself
Just give some self-love
And give myself a nudge

Step 6 – Wellness

Wellness

This section encompasses everything we have already discussed. It is about consciously being aware of your body and mind and making healthy choices towards a healthier, fulfilling life. People are a lot more aware of the word now and the need for being more conscious about it has arisen from our fast-paced lives and desk- and car-based jobs.

Work

Think about how your work affects you. If at a desk, is your posture correct? Have you thought about a standing desk? Is your chair at the right height and is the screen at the correct eye level?

If you drive a lot, do you take enough breaks? Is your wheel at the right level for you?

It is amazing how much these things can affect you. I found that I was not at the right level at my desk, I was jutting my chin forward, holding my breath (and not realizing), and grinding my teeth at night! I ended up with a lot of pain around my jaw, shoulders, and arms. Having the correct, ergonomic chair and opting for a standing desk has helped me a great deal! I tend to stand most of the day and sit in small intervals. Have a look at your work and see if you need to make any adjustments to improve your health and well-being. You can also seek professional advice from an occupational therapist if you are having great difficulty.

Self Care

Self care refers to looking after yourself and being mindful of what you need. I always make time for my daily beauty routine, and bathe in salts to relax, unwind and perform my weekly beauty routine. Yoga helps relax the mind and, if I'm feeling particularly stressed, I unwind using the 'Calm' app before bed or I read a good book.

The Calm app is a great way to introduce yourself to meditation and mindful breathing. There are many other meditation apps too, like Headspace, but you don't necessarily need an app. Just take 5 minutes to stop, slow, and watch your breath and exist in the moment. Start with 5 minutes a day and you will reap the rewards.

It's good to try and put the phone away at nighttime (sometimes tricky if you are working with different time zones like me). So, I put it on silent and face down in the corner of the living room. Its best to keep it out of your bedroom to avoid sneaky peeks at emails or messages through the night. Not to mention the blue light keeps you awake!

Sometimes I work on weekends to catch up and get myself ready for the coming week, but I set myself up for this by seating myself at my desk and readying myself to action what I see.

Seeing something that stresses you out after waking or when you are enjoying an evening with friends is the worst! It can ruin your night or morning. It has happened to me many a time, so I speak from experience.

To me, self care is also knowing when to say No to an engagement. Knowing when to listen to what your body is telling you. Maybe it is saying No to someone that drains you of your energy, or no to a task that could be given to someone else instead of trying to do everything yourself.

Self care is about staying home and hibernating for a weekend if you want to. And it's also about speaking your truth. If you don't how you feel, your thoughts can bottle up inside and make you feel uncomfortable and then appear as a physical symptom, like a sore shoulder, jaw, or feeling tired, groggy, angry, or anxious.

I personally feel like I have grown up in an era where we have so many options and we have been taught that we can do and be anything that we want which is inspiring, but for someone indecisive this can be overwhelming too. At the end of the day, you need to do what makes you happy and is line with you. If it doesn't feel right then be careful. Listen to your intuition; it is so easy to follow that nasty monkey ego and sometimes we can feel trapped.

Massage

When I was 16, I started massage training alongside my A Levels. I fell completely in love with it. This became a springboard to my career as I then studied further diplomas in Indian head massage, reflexology, theatrical and media makeup, and then a Higher National Diploma in beauty and related sciences.

I could not give up massages. I can wax myself, paint my nails, give myself a facial, even tint my eyelashes, but massage is the one thing that has so many benefits. Even though I can do an element of it myself, this is simply not the same. I believe people should fit this in to their lifestyles on a regular basis. It helps relax short and tight muscles, increase circulation and the lymphatic system, and relaxes and calms the mind, which is under so much pressure these days. We live longer, work longer, we have the drive, determination, and vision that we can do and be anything and that is exhausting!

One blissful hour of massage takes you away from that exhaustion. When was the last time you had a massage?

They use light massage and reflexology in hospitals to help patients relax, feel whole again, and relieve anxiety and depression. These are just a few of the many benefits. Touch, the transfer of energy from one to another, the ability to relax and stretch muscles and tissues is so beneficial. The body holds so much in the way of tension, stress and emotions and this can often show up as symptoms like pain or complaints like Irritable Bowel Syndrome. That sore hip, tight jaw, and those annoying headaches could be related to stress. Listen to your body as it is telling you what you need to know. Where are you tight? What aches and pains are you ignoring?

Health checks

Please make sure you keep up with your health checks, e.g. Pap smears, Prostate and skin cancer checks. If you have any niggling problems, it is best to seek advice sooner rather than leaving it until it's too late. Check, check, check, and I don't need to tell you that Dr Google, in the wrong hands, can be quite scary and untrue.

Boobs

First of all, check your boobs for any abnormalities. For more information about this you can head to the website listed at the end of this chapter: Second of all, so many ladies don't know their bra size, have never been measured, wear ill-fitting bras that can cause back pain and, of course, the dreaded sagging boobs, so see the list below for my top tips for bras.

My top tips for bras:

1. Bras should be hand-washed and air-dried. Worst case scenario is a cold wash in the washing machine in a protective net bag, but this should be avoided.
2. Don't use fabric conditioner as this is not good for the elastic.
3. How many bras you have and how often you rotate them will depend on their life span. If you only own a few, or have your favourites and wear them regularly, then they only last around 6 months, especially if you have larger boobs. Think of all that hard work for the elastic! They will last a lot longer if you take good care of them and rotate more often.
4. Get measured! People might be wearing a 36B when they are a 32D.
5. The front part of the bra should sit flat against the chest without gaping.
6. The straps should not fall off the shoulders.
7. The straps should not leave red marks on the shoulders.
8. If standing to the side, the bra be should straight around the body. If the back is riding up, it does not fit!
9. When wearing a t-shirt, your boobs should not fall out of the top of the bra and you should not see the dreaded four boobs.
10. If you have larger boobs, it is worth investing in a good bra and taking care of it, as it will help you in the long term. Better to buy a well-made, sturdy bra than three not so good bras. If you are in the DD+ range, make sure you also look for swimwear that is cup-sized.

https://www.breastcancercare.org.uk/information-support/have-i-got-breast-cancer/checking-your-breasts

Boobs

Big ones
Small ones
Round ones
Pointy ones
They come in all shapes and sizes
And all deserve prizes
You must not forget to take care
There are some tips I'd like to share
Make sure you get measured
The right fitting bra is to be treasured

You should give them a good squeeze
To put your mind at ease
Check for lumps, bumps, and changes
So you can detect anything funny in early
stages
You must also take care
Of your décolleté
Massage in some cream
This will keep your skin a dream
Not creepy and crinkly
Just smooth with no grooves
Melons, norks, jugs, tits, boobs, breasts
Whatever you want to call them
They are for life
So just adore them

Sleep

My friend (a mother) kindly pointed out that her best tip for a good nights sleep is to not have children! This list is certainly applicable to those of you who do or do not have children, however I understand you are facing an additional challenge.

1. Don't sleep with your phone. You may laugh, but people do! I actually charge mine outside of the room so that I am not tempted to take a cheeky look. Not only is the blue light bad, but what you see may stress you out: an email, a message, a Facebook post. Just ditch it! It also means you won't get distracted when you wake up.

2. It's better to have a cool room and a nice, snuggly duvet cover than be too hot, so ditch the high-heating.

3. Try to read for half an hour before bed.

4. Go to bed when you are tired. This might sound silly, but don't feel you have to go to bed if you are wide awake.

5. Try to stick to a routine of waking up and going to bed.

6. Avoid liquids a couple of hours before bed. No one wants to be getting up through the night for the toilet, so avoid if possible.

7. Avoid foods and drinks that keep you awake or are too rich. You know what they say about cheese! You don't want nightmares or acid.

8. No caffeine after 4pm. I actually have no caffeine after lunch if I can.

9. If you have anything on your mind, get it out! Write it down in a journal or a to-do list, whatever makes you feel better.

10. Never go to bed on an argument.

11. If there are certain times of the month when you feel more awake than others, check out the moon cycles! People are often more awake on a full moon and new moon. It's actually true! If you are wide awake at three, sometimes its better to just get up, write

down what's on your mind and—I am going to contradict myself here about fluid —have a herbal tea!

12.   I always find if you have exercised through the day you have a better nights sleep too. So, get walking, running, or whatever is your thing.

13.   Meditation before bed can help. Or use the Calm app and have Matthew McConaughey read you a story for bed!

Sleep tight and sweet dreams.

Step 7 – Vision Plan Travel

Vision Plan Travel

There are many books that have made an impact on me, *The Secret* is one such book. This feels cliché, but it really has. I have read it and watched the film a number of times. You must visualise yourself doing what you want and choose in life and then you become what you think.

For my wedding speech, I spoke without a piece of paper and everyone asked me how I could remember it all. I think I have always been able to do this when it comes to presentations. I went to bed every night before the wedding thinking about what I wanted to say and imagined a whole manner of things: who was there and what they would look like, how I felt, the emotions, the sunshine. And, on the day, the words just fell out of my mouth.

Life is the same as the speech I just spoke about (and not always quite so easy for me). However, when you are concise with what you want and see yourself doing, write that plan or write that list. It almost seems to appear in your life!

Whatever you do, take the time to dream about where you want to visit, where you want to live, and how you want to live. What do you want your life to include?

When I first read *The Secret*, I was single and plodding along. I was happy, but ready to meet someone and enter a new work challenge.

I produced my vision board—I wanted to travel more, work in the city, present the beauty section on QVC, see more gigs, and meet someone who liked restaurants and food as much as me! I didn't think about what he looked like. About a month later, on Friday the 13th of January, I met my now husband. A man with a hunger for travel, music, and food, and he was gorgeous! My life rapidly changed and I found myself managing a spa in Central London and travelling and eating at the best restaurants we could find, and I will never forget meeting My husband and how the vision came to life. I even ended up guest presenting for ELEMIS on QVC!

I knew the life I wanted and I found it.

So, write that plan, cut out pictures, dream of that home. If you don't believe it or take that step to make it happen, it never will.

Don't be afraid of going alone either. There is no reason why you have to take a friend or have a partner. Be comfortable in your own skin and company. As I have travelled for work and have now worked from home for 8 years, I have grown to enjoy my own company and am quite happy heading to a café to read a book or spend a few days by the pool somewhere by myself. A date with yourself can be really enjoyable and it's better than dragging someone along to something they might not want to do.

One last thing to be mindful on when thinking. Please don't dwell on what you DON'T want as this can actually attract more of what you don't want into your life. Try and stay in a positive mind set and only focus on what you do want in your life.

CONCLUSION

No one is perfect and I am not expecting or asking you to be. All I know is that a little bit of planning, decluttering of the mind and home, fueling your body with the right energy, and taking care of your precious mind—that have the power to heal—can transform how you feel on a daily basis.

Why do things that make you unhappy or unwell? As they said in the movie *Trainspotting*, 'Choose Life'. And a happy one at that. Don't put up with people that give you grief, you don't have to follow the norm and do what society says. Be a tall poppy.

Printed in the United States
By Bookmasters